About the Friend in My Heart

The Little Book of Kindness

Dipna Daryanani

Illustrated by
Sonal Gupta Vaswani

Designed by
Thematchboxgirl

Published by Red Panda, an imprint of Westland Books, a division of Nasadiya Technologies Private Limited, in 2025

No. 269/2B, First Floor, 'Irai Arul', Vimalraj Street, Nethaji Nagar, Alapakkam Main Road, Maduravoyal, Chennai 600095

Westland, the Westland logo, Red Panda and the Red Panda logo are the trademarks of Nasadiya Technologies Private Limited, or its affiliates.

Text copyright © Dipna Daryanani, 2025
Illustrations copyright © Sonal Gupta Vaswani, 2025

Dipna Daryanani asserts the moral right to be identified as the author of this work.

This is a work of fiction. Names, characters, organisations, places, events and incidents are either products of the author's imagination or used fictitiously.

ISBN: 9789371978743

10 9 8 7 6 5 4 3 2 1

All rights reserved

Printed at Nutech Print Services Pvt. Ltd.

No part of this book may be reproduced, or stored in a retrieval system, or transmitted in any form or by any means, electronic, mechanical, photocopying, recording, or otherwise, without express written permission of the publisher.

To my Nana,
whose kindness surrounds me
like a big warm hug!

I want to tell you
about the friend
in my heart.

My friend is bigger than the biggest thing you could ever imagine.

It is as **big** as this universe—gigantic and possibly infinite.

And you know what's amazing about this friend?
It just keeps on
growing
and growing
and growing.

So then, how does it fit inside my heart?

Well, my genius friend can make smaller parts of itself.
And find a warm cosy corner
in every human,
every animal,
every bird,
every wave,
every sunray,
every raindrop and
every stone's heart!

My friend loves smiles and tears of joy.
My friend loves hopping in and out of hearts.

And it makes a connection,
from one heart to the other as it hops!

Sometimes, it takes a nap.
And when it wakes up,
it loves a nice, long stretch,
making my heart expand.

Sometimes, it appears as **the feeling of care** when I feed a stray puppy.

Sometimes, it is

the feeling of generosity

when I share my favourite snack box with a friend.

The feeling of warmth,
when the winter sun feels good on my skin.

The feeling of gratitude,
when I get to enjoy a
nice and juicy mango in summer.

The feeling of affection,
when I tell my mamma, she is the prettiest.

The feeling of courage,
when I thank my teacher at the end of the class.

Sometimes, it appears as **the feeling of love,** when I say, 'I love you' to daddy, before he does.

Told you! This special friend of mine
appears in so many ways.
Oh!
Did I forget to tell you its name?
Silly me!

We call my friend …

Kindness is its name!

And do you want to know a little secret?

Kindness lives in your heart too.

'Let's take some time to remember some of the moments when you've met our friend, Kindness. Go on, grab a crayon or pencil and draw or write all the times Kindness has come visiting its cosy little den, inside your heart.

ABOUT THE AUTHOR

Dipna Daryanani is a Mumbai-based movement artist, early years educator, certified Hatha yoga practitioner, and founder of Move with Joy—a creative movement programme for young children that celebrates the body, imagination and joy of expression. She is also the co-founder of Love the World Today, a sustainable clothing brand that creates thoughtful clothing for children.

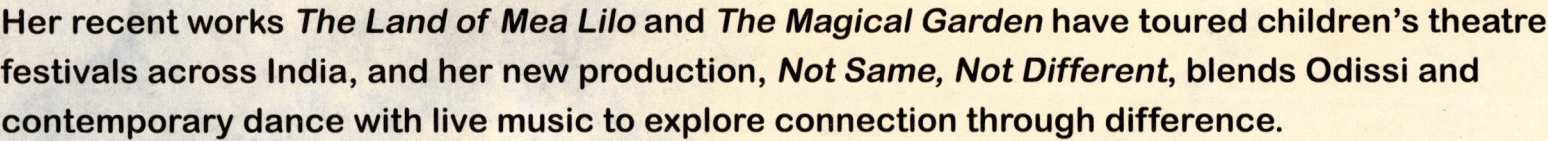

With over 17 years of experience in early childhood education and more than a decade in contemporary dance and dance-theatre, Dipna's work is grounded in the belief that kindness, curiosity and imagination are essential to learning, creating and growing. Whether in classrooms, studios or on stage, her approach centres on keeping the inner child alive—through presence, play and listening deeply to the body and the world around it.

Her recent works *The Land of Mea Lilo* and *The Magical Garden* have toured children's theatre festivals across India, and her new production, *Not Same, Not Different*, blends Odissi and contemporary dance with live music to explore connection through difference.

Dipna's interests in nature, travel, textiles and photography continue to inform her creative lens, but it is kindness that remains at the heart of everything she does, quietly shaping how she moves, teaches, creates and connects.

ABOUT THE ILLUSTRATOR

Sonal Gupta Vaswani is an artist and illustrator based in Mumbai. She has always been in love with colours and textures. Sonal loves illustrating for children as it takes her back to being a kid. She has worked on several visual books for children. When not drawing, she is talking to her cats or plants. She has grown up listening to stories by her mom and now shares the same love by conducting storytelling sessions and illustrating the stories of others. You can see more of her work at www.thematchboxgirl.com.